TEACHING
Rules!

TEACHING
Rules!

52 ways to achieve teaching success

written by **JENNY LAND MACKENZIE**

illustrated by **STEVE HICKNER**

BRIGANTINE MEDIA

Teaching Rules!

Illustrations by Steve Hickner

Brigantine Media
211 North Avenue, St. Johnsbury, Vermont 05819
Phone: 802-751-8802 | Fax: 802-751-8804
Email: neil@brigantinemedia.com
Website: www.brigantinemedia.com

ISBN 978-1-9384066-2-1

Dedication

This book is dedicated to my elementary and secondary school teachers, particularly Susanne London, Connie Metz, Carl Recchia, Joe Greenwald, David Ely, Steve Nagy, and Mary Beth Harris. Their love for their students and ingenuity in the classroom will always continue to renew and inspire me.

Acknowledgments

I would like to wholeheartedly thank my headmaster, Tom Lovett, and my colleagues at St. Johnsbury Academy. I am lucky enough to work with an outstandingly dedicated and imaginative faculty who inspire me anew each year in my teaching. Thank you to Marshall Land and to Lewis First for reading early drafts of the book and offering excellent comments. Thank you to John Rassias, Joe Greenwald, Steve Nagy, Chris Buhner, Sharon Fadden, Richard McCarthy, and Sarah Parker, whose teaching strategies inspired specific rules.

The Rules

The Rules

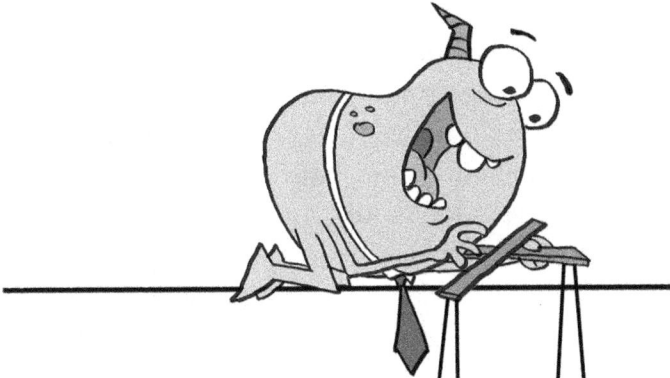

Teach your *students.*

GOOD TEACHERS ARE interested in the new students who come to their classroom every year. What makes these new students tick? What lesson plan keeps Josh involved for the whole sixty-minute class? Which test prep ideas help Ella succeed?

Only about 25 percent of your teaching time is spent on the specific subject matter. The rest is devoted to working with your students, helping them connect with the material. *You* may be teaching it for the two hundredth time, but it's completely new to everyone else in the room.

Successful teachers know that their primary job is to teach. If you want to learn more about your subject, sign up for a graduate program or switch to a research-based profession.

Being a teacher means knowing how to help students learn.

RULE
2

Take the temperature.

TAKE A BRIEF moment with each student at the start of a class.

I typically do this while checking homework. I walk around the room, look at the homework, and make sure I make a comment to each student. I answer questions I read in their journals and talk about the cartoons they draw, the graphs they make, and their choices of quotations.

The time with the students, however brief, helps me establish a one-to-one relationship with each of them. I can get a feeling for their individual

moods. A student might also mention to me, in that semi-private moment, if something is going on in his life that might affect his attention that day. If a student hasn't finished the assigned homework, I learn in that conversation if the student didn't understand my directions, if the assignment was too long or too difficult, or if the student has had an extraordinarily busy schedule.

With a clear picture of the mood and accomplishments of the class as a whole, I can tweak the homework or spontaneously adapt the activity planned for class that day. What's the use of moving on to the next concept if half the students in the room were lost on last night's homework?

A temperature check need not take more than five minutes. I let the students have that brief window of time to quietly chat with a neighbor. These five minutes don't disrupt the class. When the temperature check is done, and chatting with their neighbors worked its way out of their systems, students are ready to give their full concentration.

Assign homework first!

HOW OFTEN DID your parents tell you to do your homework first? Good advice. And I decided to apply it to my classroom.

In my first years of teaching, I had trouble with timing. I'd start to assign the homework at the end of the class and the bell would ring. Conscientious students would turn up at the end of the day to make sure they knew what to work on; others would come into class the next day and say, "I didn't hear what the homework was."

One day I had a brainstorm. Why not give the homework assignment at the beginning of class, rather than squeezing it in at the end?

The results were magical. The students were fresh and ready for direction. I put the assignment on the board, and I took time to go over it right then and there. They paid attention, they asked questions, they wrote it down. This system worked—even though the homework was based on a lesson they hadn't received yet! The homework assignment sparked the students' curiosity about what we were about to learn. They wanted to understand the new concept because they would need it to do their homework.

When you leave the homework assignment up on the board throughout the class, students can look at it during class and think about how they'll use the information when they're on their own later. Plus, when you assign the homework first, you can teach until the bell rings!

Respect your students.

"THE SECRET IN education lies in respecting the student," Ralph Waldo Emerson wrote in the nineteenth century, and that advice still holds true today.

Imagine Kevin: he's the only student in the class of twenty sixth-graders who hasn't prepared for the class project. He's let down his group. He's let you down, too, because student presentations formed your lesson plan for the day. As you're checking off those who are ready, you might feel like dropping an exasperated comment right then and there—"You know, Kevin, I'm disappointed in you today."

But put yourself in Kevin's shoes. Whether he's got a legitimate excuse or not, humiliating him in

front of his peers isn't going to take you very far in building up your student-teacher relationship and encouraging Kevin to hold to his commitments next time. It is possible that he has a reasonable or even serious reason that he didn't get his homework done, regardless of his past performance.

No matter how angry you feel with a student, or however sure you are that you have the right answer in a given situation, be sure to take a step back and realize that you're talking to another person. And that young person deserves as much respect as anyone else you work with, including your supervisor or your colleagues. When students of any age feel part of a two-way conversation—that their opinion and perspective matters—you open up the possibility for changes in behavior so that real learning can take place.

Model the love of learning.

THE GREAT AMERICAN education reformer Horace Mann said, "A teacher who is attempting to teach without inspiring the pupil with a desire to learn is hammering on cold iron."

But how, specifically, does a teacher inspire the pupil?

One way is to show students that you enjoy the activity. Model what you want them to do. As an English teacher, I frequently assign warm-up writing exercises at the beginning of class. I've found that reluctant students participate more eagerly if they see me chewing my pencil and scribbling, too. They're more willing to share their writing in class if they watch me read aloud something I just wrote.

During independent reading time, I read a book of my own that fits the criteria I've set up for the students. They want to know what I'm reading, and they get excited to tell me about the books they have chosen.

When you share an activity with your students, you're not only building classroom community, you're inspiring students to try something new and take a risk.

Think across disciplines.

PHYSICS AND ENGLISH Literature—little in common, right?

Wrong.

Last year, I ended up with a group of self-identified science geeks in a compulsory literature course. Over the summer, I approached the

Physics teacher to see if our classes could overlap in reading Mary Shelley's *Frankenstein*. He agreed. My class read the book, while his class had discussions about the science behind the text and the relevancy to ethical questions in science today. Small groups drawn from both classes wrote a creative piece based on scientific research, with a bibliography, that dramatized an ethical question related to a current scientific issue. The groups presented their writing to each other and submitted their pieces for review in the school literary journal. The result? The science-lovers in my class carried their interest in the unit to the texts we studied next. The humanities-thinkers in the physics class developed a greater understanding of the relevancy of scientific thought on culture and creative expression.

This method works for elementary students as well. For example, when studying ecosystems and changing seasons, look at scientific cycles—but also find poetry or artwork that portrays the process in a metaphorical way. Read aloud a book of fiction on the same topic. Ask a colleague with a special background in another discipline to come into your classroom to share his scientific or creative perspective.

Connecting curriculum across disciplines helps students have those "Aha!" moments.

Change up the leadership.

IT'S THE FIRST week of class. You're ready to divide the class into small groups. Whom do you pick to be group leader? Eva, the girl with her hand up in the air, or Zach, the boy melting into the back corner?

The answer: both of them. Both need to try being the leader at different times.

Zach might not be ready to take on the challenge during the first week of school, but you can let him know that you'll expect him to build up to it, and that everyone will be taking turns in the leadership position. Give him some scaffolding with smaller jobs where you single him out in a less public way. Maybe he can start to take responsibility by giving him a special task with homework,

such as looking up a particular fact and reporting back to his group.

If you switch around the leaders often and give students multiple small opportunities to try out the role, they'll be less likely to freeze up when it's their turn to lead.

Plug into the power of Day One.

START OFF THE year with the right impression! On Day One of class, you're setting the stage for all the months to come. Think carefully about how to make the most of the first day of class.

May

April

March

February

January

December

November

October

September

- Learn the students' names—immediately. Look up the students ahead using the online administration system. Let the students personalize nametags for their desks. Use eye contact and call on specific students right away. Using the names will help you memorize them quickly. Even more importantly, the students will pay attention and they'll learn that you care about them as individuals.

- Spend some time letting the students get acquainted with each other. Even if most of the students know each other from the previous year, you'll want new students to feel comfortable as quickly as possible. You'll also want to establish that this is a new group in a new year. Tie the activity to class material. For example, get them to describe their favorite scientist to a partner. Ask students to introduce the partner and their selected scientist to the class.

- Lay down some ground rules: how you will collect assignments; how you will give them feedback; what kinds of tests they can expect. Let them know what's important to you about their work and attitude, so that the class immediately becomes a shared experience.

- Give them a taste of your teaching style. You'll have a lot to tell them, but they'll tune out if they hear about too many logistics at once! Start teaching in an active way that sets up the work to come, creates a sense of community, and helps the students get to know you and the group of other students in the room.

Think about what your new students will be telling their parents at the supper table that night about their first class with you. Convince both student and parents that it will be a worthwhile and fun year ahead!

Develop a routine.

YOU'RE LOOKING AT a blank teacher's schedule book. It's your job to decide what will go on in class every single day. How can you organize those endless weeks?

The solution: break your syllabus into a weekly schedule. It will make your planning easier, and your students will love having a predictable workweek. Second graders will look forward to knowing that they will have time reading stories with you after lunch each day. High school students can make plans if they can count on a schedule. Choose a day (say, Tuesdays) where you introduce the concept of the week. Build in some practice time or a game on Wednesdays. On Thursday, give the quiz. This kind of weekly planning not only helps the students, it helps the teacher by filling in a lot of your calendar. Then add in the units that make up the course, specific lesson plans, and the long-term projects.

This method works for your daily plan, too. Once you have a firm bedrock for the consistent parts of your class each day (homework check, new material, quizzes, etc.), you'll be able to go back and fill in the not-so-big-blanks in your day-to-day syllabus, creating the detailed plans that lead to successful lessons.

We're creatures of habit . . . and students are, too!

Keep the questions coming.

In their theory of inquiry education developed in the 1960s, Neil Postman and Charles Weingartner advocated: "Once you have learned to ask questions—relevant and appropriate and substantial questions—you have learned how to learn and no one can keep you from learning whatever you want or need to know."

How do you develop this skill in your students? Make sure *you* are asking questions all the time, in various ways. See who understands a concept before you start teaching. Show students a diagram or a picture and ask if they can explain it. Organize a formal Socratic circle and ask students to engage in exercises of dialogue and

listening. Socrates believed that all thinking comes from asking questions. As a teacher, more than imparting knowledge, you're trying to get your students to learn to think critically and independently. You're teaching them to ask questions.

If you ask questions of all of your students, rather than just calling on one or two students for emphasis between major points, your class will begin to see this type of participation as a crucial part of learning. Shy students won't dread being called on when they see that all students are being called on each day. Find ways to use their answers (whether correct or not) to lead to further discussion, even as you point out the right answer. This will help students feel positive about their contributions.

As the old saying goes, "There are no stupid questions . . ."

Rule the clock.

TIME IN THE classroom can get away from you very quickly, especially on days where students are working or presenting in small groups. How do you control the clock to get through all of the material you need to cover before the bell rings?

Solution One: Think in modules. Break up the group work into small chunks: planning, constructing, presenting, debriefing. Allow adequate time for each section. If you're runnning out of time for valuable reflection, schedule the debriefing—and maybe even the presenting—at the start of the next class.

Solution Two: Watch the clock. Before the class starts, give a student who needs leadership practice the job of being timekeeper. When you are juggling the needs of so many students, it's easy to lose track of time. Have a student let you know periodically how much time has elapsed, so you can cut off a long-winded group that is taking more than its fair share. Don't forget to give your student timekeeper plenty of praise for a simple but important job.

Solution Three: Check the temperature. Every twenty minutes, ask the students how they're doing and if they need more time. Make a reasonable call based on their efforts. If they've worked hard on a project, each group will want enough time to present. It may be better to cut off an activity and renew it the next day. Bonus: you'll gain the added benefit of having a good excuse to review the previous day's material before you resume the presentations.

Make every minute count!

Promote process over product.

HAVE YOU EVER watched as a student receives back an assignment that you've marked—how she flips straight to the end to see the grade, ignoring all your well-considered comments?

Here are a few ways to help students focus on the process of learning rather than the final numerical score assigned to their work:

1 In your rubrics, build rewards for all aspects of the work. A student might perform well in some areas, even if the overall grade is not stellar. For example, for a history oral report,

**GRADES
with
COMMENTS**

**GRADES
ONLY**

you can let Eva know that she has not yet proven that she can refer accurately to her sources, but that she deserves high marks for her oral delivery of the material.

2   When you complete a project or a task in class, ask students to take a moment for self-reflection. Younger students can take turns speaking up to comment on their strengths and places for improvement. Then you can give them both parallel comments and perhaps offer slightly different criticism. Older students can take a quiet moment to write a short reflection. If possible, let them hand in the reflection with their final written work or at the time of a final group or individual presentation. I have found that most students will give an accurate assessment of their strengths and weaknesses. Praise them for developing into strong self-critics and ask them to use these self-identified markers to improve on the next assignment.

3   Allow students to revise their work for a better grade or give them a second opportunity to demonstrate their skill in a certain area. That way the grade will become a part of the process of learning, rather than an end product.

When students focus on their process of development, they are more likely to take pride in and responsibility for the end result.

Hold the conference *before* the assignment.

I WAS TEACHING basic English Literature to soph-
omores. In our student-teacher conference after the
first assignment, Turner came in after school with a
sullen frown on his face. He hadn't given any evidence for proof in his first paper, although we'd gone
over how to accomplish the task. I tried to show him
where he had started off well and where he could
have added more information, so that he could do
better on the next assignment. I was focusing on the
positives, right?

Not from Turner's perspective! "What's the point?" he asked me in a surly tone. "I can't redo this assignment."

So I tried a new tactic. I abandoned the previous paper and moved on to the next assignment that was due. We sat side-by-side brainstorming new ideas, new ways of approaching the evidence. Turner went home with the essay half-written, and he returned with a finished paper. He earned the first "A" he'd ever received on an English essay.

Turner started coming in regularly *before* an assignment was due. By the end of the semester, he'd earned his first "A" in high school. He even signed up for an elective English class the next year. He started smiling in class and making constructive contributions because he loved the positive feedback from me and from his classmates.

Feedback is often too late when it's given after the assignment. Think like a coach and offer encouragement *before* they start the game.

Root, root, root for the home team!

START THINKING ABOUT your class as a team
and the students as players. The team needs to work
together to perform its best. Some students will have
more natural talent and advantages than others, but
when it's a team, everyone contributes to its success.

When your class is a team, you need to be the
cheering squad on both the individual and group
level. Offer enthusiastic praise whenever a student
has achieved a new level in terms of homework, class
activities, collaboration, or even behavior. Make it
public: "Thanks, Ethan, for stepping up as the leader
of your group today!" and "Super job, Courtney,
on going the extra mile with your homework last

night—look how much it's paid off in class today!" and "Remember how well Duncan explained the concept of biofeedback to us yesterday?"

Don't save successes for private moments; share them front and center. I recognize individuals often, and try to spread the wealth so no one feels embarrassed or singled out. They are happy that someone noticed their work. Make sure to praise the class as a whole when you can: "Give yourselves a pat on the back—this week, every member of the class got the essays in on time!"

The more cheering you give, the better the team is going to want to perform!

RULE
15

Admit mistakes.

THE ANCIENT CHINESE philosopher Confucius said, "The essence of knowledge is, having it, to apply it; not having it, to confess your ignorance."

When you make a mistake, admit it! You're wrong! You're never going to earn your students' respect by standing your ground when you make an error. Instead, make it a teaching moment: you're still learning, too! Give the student credit for her knowledge; use it as an opportunity to increase the student's sense of self-worth. "You're absolutely right, Tricia. My mistake. You read that section of the book last night even more

$$\begin{array}{r} 2 \\ +\,2 \\ \hline 5 \end{array}$$

carefully than I did!" Or, "Well, Ryan, I don't have an answer right now. I'm not sure what current thinking suggests about the reasons for bee colony collapse. Why don't I look into it and get back to you tomorrow?" Then, of course, make yourself a reminder to do the research!

Remember, you're a teacher, not an encyclopedia—you don't need to know everything. Your willingness to admit your occasional error will promote a shared sense of commitment to honesty and the process for learning.

The exit ticket.

EDUCATIONAL GURU ROBERT Marzano has developed one of the most effective teaching tools imaginable to the profession: the exit slip.

Always try to save a few minutes at the end of class for students to reflect on what they learned that day. You'll help your students focus and remember what they've learned; they'll think about the key points of information and make connections with it. You can give students a brief written quiz, no points attached, or better yet, ask students to let you know something new they learned that day. You'll find out where your strengths—and weaknesses—were as a teacher that day, and you'll discover what you need to clear up in your planning for the next lesson. Think about it as the second temperature check of the class—you take one at the beginning to see how homework went and what you need to cover, and you take one at the end to anticipate what kind of instruction will need to happen next. You'll find out which activities the students are enjoying the most. You'll also help them cement the purpose of the day's work in their minds.

Envision your classroom community.

WHEN POSSIBLE, DESIGN your lesson plans after you know what your mix of students will be.

Here are some of the issues I consider: How old are these students? What is the mix of students in the class, in terms of gender, socioeconomic background, and cultural diversity? What approach to the major course concepts might appeal to that mix of students?

A couple of years ago, I was given the new charge to teach Accelerated English to seniors. I did some research before the term started, checking with the guidance office and other teachers, and I learned quite a bit of information. This class would have more boys than girls. The students preferred math and science courses to English courses; they were

taking honors-level courses in the other fields. The ESL students in the class were highly motivated to be in an accelerated class.

I used this information about the students to envision a class that looked at literature from the standpoint of scientific and ethical inquiry. I set a goal that all students would become more confident writers and see the relevance of writing to the fields that interested them. From Day One, I let them acknowledge openly that they might prefer and excel at other subjects—and I asked them to work as a team towards making the learning in *this* course fun, meaningful, and relevant to their goals beyond high school.

Know your students and tailor your lessons to what makes them tick.

Let the kids build the rubrics.

HOW MANY TIMES have you heard a student say, "The teacher GAVE ME a bad grade! It's not fair!"?

It's a step forward to let students know how you will grade their work by sharing clear rubrics. It's an even bigger and better step to let students take part in building those rubrics.

Let's say you're creating a rubric for oral book reports to be given by your fourth graders throughout the year. Ask your class to help decide the fair categories for assessment. Students might mention delivery, preparation, and quality of visuals. What would an adequate performance in each of these categories look like? How could it exceed that standard? Have the students make a colorful classroom poster that reminds them they "own" the rubric.

As a teacher, you will want to have most of the say on grading standards, but you can help the students understand the marking scale. You can give students a say in what practices contribute to meeting the standards. When working with state-mandated assessments, let the students take a look at those, too, in simplified form.

When you're evaluating creative work, which students feel is more personal, you're much more likely to have buy-in to the final grade if the students feel that they've helped create the assessment.

Teachers know that they don't *give* grades—students *earn* them. Involve your students in building rubrics so they know where their grades come from.

Ask for help.

STUCK IN A rut? Need a new method of teaching the carbon cycle? Not sure how to breathe excitement into math facts?

You can find plenty of ideas in teacher's journals. You can go online and look for advice. You can get professional development credit by attending a workshop.

But first, ask other teachers you know to share activities from their personal bags of tricks. Richard, another member of our English department, teaches many of the same classes that I do. He makes an effort to drop off effective new lesson plans that he's tried out; he also asks me for help with

his problems. Your colleagues are solving the same types of issues you have. Why not go to them for advice?

In a digital world, it feels faster to go online and search for ideas when you're looking for a teaching solution. But don't forget to take time to chat with your peers—you'll be rewarded both with good ideas and the pleasure of getting to know your colleagues!

Take time for you!

ACCORDING TO A 2015 survey conducted by the Association of Teachers and Lecturers in the U.K., 76 percent of first-year teachers and trainees have seriously contemplated leaving the profession due to the heavy workload. Every teacher needs to balance the demands of the job with his/her own personal life.

Here's what I do: Make time every day for an activity you enjoy—and stick to your plan. Join a group for indoor soccer. Find a local quiz night. My headmaster asked why I hadn't burned out after three years like many other young teachers in my cohort. I told him that I love teaching, but I also love other activities. Those activities help me connect with the community outside the school.

Turn your after-school duties into fun activities for you. If you need regular exercise in your day, volunteer as an assistant coach for a team and take students out on running loops. If you love theater but there's already an established drama program in place, start an improv club.

Make time for the things and people you love.

Bring your interests to school.

IF YOU ASK my twin daughters what they remember best about kindergarten, they'll tell you about the fun they had learning about China. They learned to write simple characters, tried on traditional clothing, celebrated Chinese holidays and ate Chinese dishes using chopsticks.

China is not included in our state standards for kindergarten. But their kindergarten teacher, Ms. Potter, had adopted a young Chinese girl and taken a leave year for the two of them to live in China. Once back home, Ms. Potter brought her passion, as well as her treasure trove of cultural goodies, into the classroom to stimulate learning.

This year, at a new school, both girls

eagerly signed up for Mandarin Club. I'm thrilled that they have had such a joyous beginning to learning about the world and other languages.

Make your interests your students' interests, too. Your enthusiasm for the subject will be contagious.

Take field trips.

WHILE THE HEART of teaching may take place within the four walls of the classroom, meaningful visits to real places outside of school turn experience into learning. My students who graduated ten years ago still drop me notes saying, "Remember that trip to Rudyard Kipling's house? I'll never forget it!" I don't mind when other teachers take some of my students on trips to Quebec to practice French or to the Boston Science Museum to view an exhibition—and your peers won't begrudge your taking their students on rare occasions, either.

Field trips don't have to be expensive. A trip exploring rotting logs in a nearby forest can help bring life science lessons to life. A field trip can be a special film shown in the school library—bring the beanbag chairs and popcorn.

If you have a limited budget, plan a class trip with other teachers. This will give you an excuse to forge collaborative ideas with your colleagues. You'll be more likely to secure the funds and support you need from your school if you make requests ahead and tie the trip firmly to classroom assignments.

Bon voyage!

Ditch the plan.

YOU'RE READY FOR the next class of students. You know exactly what you've planned for today and you're well prepared. But before class begins, Lizzie walks in full of excitement about a book she finished last night. Ditch the plan for a few minutes—let her do an impromptu book report to share that passion with the other students.

You've planned an activity with small groups of four students, but they've all got the Friday giggles and can't stay on task. Time to quickly shift the activity to a whole-group learning game so you can keep eye contact with everyone and keep the class focused.

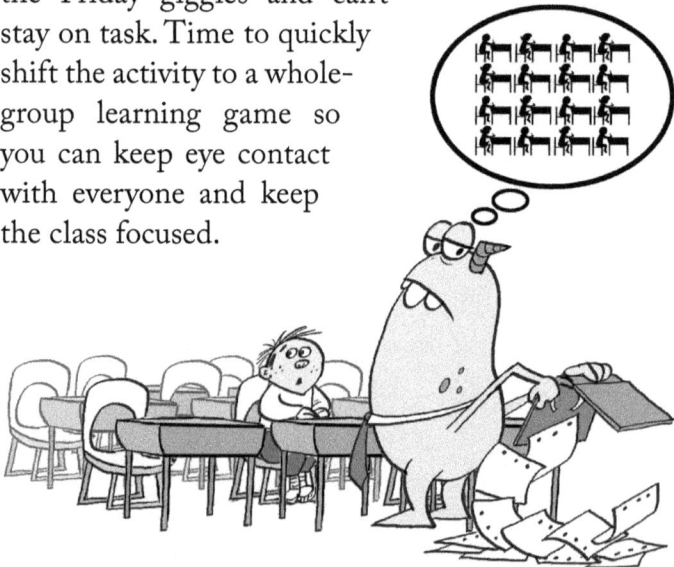

You show up on Monday ready to give out the week's vocabulary words, but half the class is out on a field trip. Save that work for tomorrow, and take advantage of the small group size to have a spirited debate on an interesting topic, or have in-depth conferences with students. Use the small size of the class to draw out a shy student who will be less intimidated to take on a leadership role because there are fewer students around.

Have a plan—but be prepared to improvise when something unexpected comes your way.

Enjoy what you teach.

ON MY FIRST day of Latin 1, my teacher announced to the class, "Latin is not my first love." Mr. Smith was a French teacher, but his department had told him that he needed to add a Latin class to his schedule.

Although I usually loved school, I wrote off Latin from the first hour. If my teacher wasn't interested in the subject, why would I like it? Mr. Smith assigned exercises from the textbook in class and more of the same for homework. Mr. Smith made Latin boring.

Compare my Latin experience with that of students two towns away. Their Latin teacher created toga events, taught the students to sing carols in Latin, and held contests to stimulate

learning declensions and vocabulary. Those students had fun. And I'm sure their teacher did, too.

Sometimes you have to teach a subject that is not your favorite. But find a way to enjoy the subject, because that spark will energize your students.

RULE
25

Ditch the textbooks.

ONE OF THE saddest sights I have ever seen is a first grade class full of disengaged children plodding through a list of problems in a textbook. What a bore!

The best teachers design hands-on projects and written work with examples students connect with through their own experiences.

The math department chair at our high school recently made the radical move of banning textbooks as the center of the syllabi for our math teachers. It's a tremendous amount of work for the teachers—creating all the lessons, activities, quizzes, and homework assignments.

But the students love the change. Class feels

relevant and student-centered. Activities have more spark and ingenuity. The teachers are engaged, too, because they're teaching to their strengths. There can be a place for supplementary work or readings drawn from textbooks. But textbooks shouldn't be the primary way you dispense information.

Many schools require teachers to use specific textbooks. If your school does, add your own individual activities to make class more exciting and relevant for your students.

RULE
26

Display class work.

MY HARDEST MOMENT of teaching was my first morning in my classroom, before my first group of students arrived. Entering halfway through the year, there was no budget for spiffing up the classroom. I stared at the empty walls and couldn't imagine spending hours in this sterile room. I couldn't imagine how my students could ever feel at home in it, either.

So I let the kids do the work. We got out the markers, paper, and glue, and the students showed me who they were through personalized collages. Over time, I've learned to create assignments purposefully connected to class material that give tactile and visual stimulation as well as brighten the walls. I pin colorful paper or fabric on the bulletin boards as a background and then get out the supplies. Students love working with their hands, whether they are kindergarteners or seniors in high school.

The classroom is *their* room, so let them make it their own! Show them that you're proud of their work, and point it out from time to time. The room will change visually from year to year, keeping you as fresh as the students when a new school year rolls around.

RULE
27

Keep parents in the loop.

MOST TEACHERS DON'T enjoy having to call a parent. It's not usually good news, and it takes time in the evening.

But my friend Andrew, a veteran teacher, has learned that communication with parents can be the key to success for some students. He makes it a point to call at least two parents a week, for a variety of reasons—to pass along information about unsatisfactory performance, to praise a project well executed, or just to see if the parent has any questions. Over the course of one semester, he contacts a parent of every student at least once.

It's a smart idea, and one I've adopted. I have learned that many parents are reluctant to initiate dialogue with their child's teacher but are happy to hear from me, whether I am calling with praise or criticism. If there are issues about homework completion or behavior, parents really appreciate a phone call early in the school year, rather than halfway through the marking period, so they can follow up at home.

Your students' parents are a big factor in your students' success—don't be afraid to keep in touch with them.

Learn each student's story.

FORTY-YEAR TEACHING veteran Rita Pierson proclaimed in a 2013 education TED talk that "every child needs a champion—an adult who will never give up on them, who understands the power of connection and insists that they become the best that they can possibly be." You need to know your students well if you want to give them that kind of support.

Try to develop a connection with each student from the moment you meet your class. On Day One, ask the students to give you personal information.

Besides their names and parent contact information, ask them about their favorite classes and activities at school, the parts of your class that they're looking forward to and the parts that they're most worried about, and what they enjoy doing after school.

I always ask my students to write down something they'd like to try that they've never done before. The responses range from the usual (bungee jump, travel to other continents) to the much less predictable. One boy wrote that he'd always dreamed of taking a ballet class. I told him I'd help him write a college essay on the subject—as long as he called me after his first ballet class at his dream school the following year. Sure enough, the next September, I got the happy phone call.

You never quite know who is sitting in front of you and what is important to each student until you ask.

RULE
29

Celebrate successes outside
the classroom.

"HEY, LET'S GIVE it up for Carrie—did you hear about her awesome ski race yesterday?"

This might not sound like part of a math lesson where every minute counts, especially for a student who has missed countless days due to illness and races, but it's certainly a critical moment in the life of a classroom.

Spend a moment or two during each class giving praise for your students' accomplishments outside the classroom. Ask Sylvia about her lacrosse game. Ask Joe about opening night of the school play. Ask Matt

about his project for the recycling club. Depending on the nature of the accomplishment, you can recognize the student with a statement directed at the whole class or give it one-on-one. Either way, focusing on their lives outside the classroom helps students understand that you care about them as individuals.

Make the most of Parents' Night.

PARENTS' NIGHT TAKES a lot of energy. It often takes place not very many weeks into the year as a school open house. You want to show you are organized, enthusiastic, and well prepared. Will you be able to remember each of your students and their individual needs and accomplishments when their parents ask specific questions?

Here's how to make the most of the big night.

First, be prepared. Have handouts ready with your contact information and any notes about the subject matter you will be covering in the class. Pass out web addresses that link parents to student homework and class information. If you've made handouts for the students at the beginning of the term with this information, you can just make copies of those. (Hint: make the extra copies right at the start of the term and have them waiting on your shelf. You'll be all ready to go!) If you have students on IEP plans, be sure to review that information so it is fresh in your mind before you meet with the parents. Have a folder with hard copies of the plans right in front of you.

Second, take notes at Parents' Night. You'll have valuable conversations with parents where they may suggest strategies that could help their child in the classroom. You might think you'll remember, but you see a lot of parents in one night, so the notes will really help keep all the new information at your fingertips.

Share your students' passions.

GEORGE BERNARD SHAW wrote, "I'm not a teacher: only a fellow traveler of whom you asked the way. I pointed ahead—ahead of myself as well as you."

Once in a while, seize the opportunity for a one-on-one moment of discovery with a student. If a student comes into class with a new passion for learning about stars and galaxies, offer to do some research together. Help her special-order a book in the school library. Help her find a video, and watch it with her after school if you can. If a student has a passion for cooking, offer to swap recipes and compare notes on how to measure and tweak ingredients. If a student shows great interest in ecology, connect her to a bird count at the local Audubon Center, and offer to join in, too. If a student adores a current sci-fi series, offer to read the latest novel along with him so you can chat about it together.

As teachers, we're always telling students what they will be learning. How exciting—for you and your students—to have them bring the topics to you!

Make an anti-procrastination pact.

STUDENTS WANT COMMENTS on their work in a timely fashion. But you have multiple students to grade and plenty of planning to do for tomorrow. How do you get comments back to your students quickly?

Remember, you're in the driver's seat. You can usually decide when assignments come in. Do you have more time at the beginning of the week? Set a grading night on Tuesdays. Do you prefer to grade at a more leisurely pace over the weekend? Ask for their journals on Friday afternoons.

Make it a rule of thumb to turn around any assignments within a week. From the

Tomorrow File

student's perspective, comments are more relevant when they still have a clear memory of their work. Plus, you need to give the feedback before they begin the next assignment.

Strike a deal with your students. Let them know that you will give them enough time to complete the assignment and that you expect it turned in on time. They can hold you accountable for getting your comments back to them within a week. They will begin to understand that homework is a two-way promise, a dialogue between teacher and student.

Communicate regularly with the Learning Services department.

EVEN WITH THE best intentions, it's easy to forget to keep the Learning Services department informed about your students who have extra accommodations as outlined in their IEP plans. But it's very important to do it. If you keep communication constant with each student's case manager, those students are more likely to succeed.

Designate a time of the day or week to send updates. I've found that writing individual e-mails

to each case manager is incredibly laborious, so I create an e-mail list to all the managers with whom I'm working in a given semester. Whenever I give a report, I list the initials of each child I'm working with who needs that extra attention, and give a very brief report. Here's an example:

LM   Did not hand in homework today; 2 days behind.

CR   Huge difficulty grasping how to use notes to write an outline.

PD   Great day! Spoke up in class!

SA   Minor confrontation with another student. Call me if you need details.

This type of communication takes time. But it's critical. The case manager will use those notes to give the student the individualized attention that he/she needs.

Bite off a little at a time.

IN MY FIRST year of teaching, Gabe was one of my better students. He usually turned in thoughtful essays that met the goals of each assignment. But when we did a unit on research, he handed in an inferior paper. He used fewer sources than required, and his paper showed a lack of organization. He submitted a paper that wasn't even close to the required length. When I

pulled him aside for a quiet after-school conference, I found that he felt anxious about writing a paper of that length and magnitude. Although Gabe was smart and knew how to write, he needed far more help with organization than I had offered him.

The solution: step-by-step, bite-size assignments. Next time, the first assignment was writing introductory arguments, and then we examined them in class. Then I gave feedback orally to small groups and asked students to revise the arguments for the next night's homework.

Another idea that works is to have students prepare an outline for their upcoming essay, and then ask peers to give a review based on a checklist. Where possible, build these in-between assignments into class work and use the building blocks as a class activity.

Assignments broken into manageable chunks help students achieve success at a higher rate.

RULE
35

Build the due dates around *your* schedule.

THIS SHOULD BE an obvious strategy for teachers—but as a first year teacher, I didn't realize it. I felt that I had to give assignment due dates based on rigid work schedules for students and on the hard-and-fast deadlines of the marking periods.

My department chair pointed out the virtues of flexibility. Even though I might need an end-of-unit essay test or project grade by the end of the marking period, I certainly did not need to make the end of the unit happen right in the very final days of the semester. He recommended that I stagger projects so

that I had plenty of time to turn around all of the assignments and still be able to write narrative report cards. If I finished my end-of-semester grading early, I could start a new unit that would carry on in the next semester. Near the end of the final marking period of the year, when all units must be completed, I could make the final assessment an oral report that I could score and give feedback in class, to free up time to give final grades.

It's amazing how a small shift in timing can contribute so much to teacher well-being!

RULE
36

Make it a contest!

SOME OF MY favorite-ever experiences as a kid in the classroom came from teachers who created contests.

In tenth grade, my English teacher, Joe Greenwald, designed the Grammar Olympics. We played Participle and Gerund *Twister*, threw free throws as bonus points in Comma Basketball, and ran races to the blackboard to fix errors in parallelism. And instead of slogging through worksheets made by anonymous teachers hundreds of miles away, we practiced our skills using worksheets written by our peers (with funny inside class jokes to keep us motivated) and vetted by our teacher.

Mr. Greenwald's Olympic games live on in my classroom. I've learned that contests—especially ones designed by the students themselves—keep the class engaged and active.

When you develop classroom games, be sure that you're thinking hard about the learning potential as well as the entertainment value of the activities. When working with high schoolers, I let the students create the games and help them tweak them to fit a lesson plan. When working with younger students, design the games yourself. I ask students what their favorite games are—*Sorry!*, *Chutes and Ladders*, *Jeopardy!*, baseball—and create learning games modeled on those.

You're trying to offer the students practice opportunities, so games where students are eliminated are not the best choice. Opt for games that establish winners based on cumulative points. Play plenty of rounds and mix up the groups so that everybody has a chance to win.

Review comments in person.

You've stayed up half the night putting comments on student papers. The next day, you hand the papers back. The students quickly flip to the back of the paper, look at the grade, and stuff the paper into their folders, never to emerge again. You think, "but wait—read the comments!"

Here's a different strategy. Take a short but focused amount of time in class for your students

Nice job. Keep it up.

to read the comments and ask you questions. You can walk around the room, asking individual students if they understand the comments and if they make sense. This process should take only about five minutes.

I know it works for elementary students, too. My seven-year-old twins have begun to write their first short take-home essays for English, history, and science this year. Each week, their teacher hands back the assignment with written comments and briefly discusses the comments with each student. That way, the teacher's message is very clear. As a parent, I can read the comments with my kids at home to help them apply the comments to next week's work.

If your school uses tablets or another system where papers are submitted online, you may find that you and your students miss this opportunity to review comments together. Ask your students to take out their iPads in class and review the comments while you are there to answer their questions.

There's no substitute for person-to-person contact.

Give students a choice of assessment.

ALL GOOD TEACHERS try to develop activities to best assess students' skills. But what if the activities don't fit well with a particular student's skill set? On some assignments, let your students decide how they will be assessed.

Maybe Noah knows the material, but he can't organize his thoughts well on paper. Give him the option of an oral assessment if he can speak well.

Students will feel they have some control over their assignment. As a result, they're more likely to care about the quality of their performance.

Letting your students choose the assessment on some class activities doesn't undermine your authority—it creates a culture of two-way respect.

Set limits for grading.

GRADING ESSAYS TAKES so much time! I like to write plenty of comments on my students' work, but there are not enough hours in the day to always do as thorough a job as I'd like. Over the years, I've developed a few ways to keep this task within a manageable timeframe.

1   Restrict written comments to an agreed-upon set of parameters. You can set those

parameters with the individual students ("Sam, we're going to look at this essay just in terms of organization.") or with the class as a whole ("Write a really tight opening argument. That's going to be the main focus of the assignment for everyone this time."). There's a plus here for the student, too—it's easier to process comments focusing on just a couple of critical areas.

2 Let the students peer review work the day before the big assignment is due. Give them time to take the drafts home for revisions before you see the final product. If they've peer reviewed effectively, you should be looking at better essays that require fewer comments.

3 Give the students multiple opportunities to craft essays over a two-week period, workshop them in class, and then ask them to pick out their top essay for you to grade. Students will get more practice writing essays and you're likely to read their best work.

When you use grading as a teaching and learning tool, you'll limit the amount of time you'll need to spend, and students will usually produce better work —a win for everyone!

Let the kids teach.

REMEMBER THE DRONING teacher in the Charlie Brown TV specials? "Wah wah wah wah wah . . ." No wonder poor Peppermint Patty could never figure out what was going on in class. And while there's certainly a time and a place for a well-designed, energetic lecture, most educators agree that students learn best through hands-on, experiential learning.

What do you do when you need to convey hard-core facts and concepts? Or the background information to a new unit?

Try assigning your students to teach the new material, either singly or in very small groups. Develop presentation skills with small speaking assignments early in the year, well before you get to the student teaching.

Divide students into small groups to prepare lessons for each other. For example, students could work in groups to teach the steps of the water cycle. Give students plenty of ideas how to capture the audience's attention (questions, short exercises, relevant humor). The presenters will gain valuable speaking skills and enjoy being experts on the assigned topic. With support from you, they'll enjoy working with their peers and pay attention to all the presentations.

No more "wah wah"!

RULE
41

Keep it moving!

PIONEERING FOREIGN LANGUAGE educator John Rassias believed in movement at the heart of the classroom experience. Even at the college level, his students leapt over desks and twirled around in improvisatory reenactments of moments of ancient history and theatre using his method of learning languages.

Well-planned physical activity helps keep students engaged. I'm a big fan of desks that can be moved around. Some days when we're trying to plow through lots of detailed information, I'll ask the students to pick up their desks and move into small circles, then back into large ones. They learn better when their perspective in the classroom is changing on a physical level and if they shift to working with

different groups. Sometimes I'll ask the students to do a project with artwork on the floor. I'll ask them to break into small groups to find a way to act out a concept to teach to the class. After they move, they are ready to refocus on the work ahead.

Keep yourself moving, too—it will keep your students more interested in what you're saying if they focus on you in different parts of the room at different times. Stand up, kneel down, go sit next to a student.

Research shows that children and adults aren't healthy when they're sitting all day. Get moving!

RULE
42

Make time for peer review.

ALWAYS KEEP IN mind one of the most valuable resources in the room—your other students. If you schedule in enough highly structured peer review exercises on a regular basis, students will become proficient at delivering meaningful criticism, and they won't feel put on the spot when asked to share their work. Eventually, your students will become better self-critics.

Here's how this can work for most grade levels and subject matter:

Imagine a fifth-grade class learning how to organize notes into an outline. You ask the students to bring in their outlines and let them know ahead that they'll be taking part in peer review. Post a list of short questions for the peer reviewer, such as, "Is there an introduction?" Is the outline broken up into logical categories?

When seventh-grade students give an oral presentation in biology class, ask the class to mark them according to the rubric, as you will be doing.

Give each peer reviewer paper with space for two commendations and two recommendations. Use the exercise as a way to figure out the needs of the class, then base the rest of your lesson around remediation for those points.

Even young students are able to make simple comments about others' work, and when you structure the review process, the results will be enlightening for everyone.

RULE
43

Change it up to keep it fresh.

YOU'VE BEEN TEACHING for a few years— you've developed a rhythm and a bag of tricks, from creating daily lesson plans, to figuring out the grading system.

But how do you keep your teaching fresh?

Don't try changing everything for the sake of change, or resting back on what you know. Take a middle approach. Reflect back on your successes. If something worked particularly well last year, leave it in place. But also take a hard look at what might have gone more smoothly. If some part of your teaching was lackluster, invest your efforts in one new project. If you teach elementary school, try developing a new science curriculum that's tied to some local resources that you've never taken advantage of before. If you

teach high school, try creating a new unit for just one course to revive the syllabus.

When you meet your new students, you'll feel energized about your new project, and that enthusiasm will carry over to your students. At the same time, you'll have enough pieces in place that you won't feel overwhelmed with the coming of the new school year.

Set the ground rules for speaking out.

PICTURE A CLASSROOM with lively discussion, where the students feel comfortable sharing stories and engaging in on-topic conversation. How do you encourage a vibrant environment where students feel safe taking verbal risks?

Set up guidelines for conversation in your first days of class. I ask my students to wait until the speaker has finished before raising their hands. I also ask students to consider whether a comment is relevant to the lesson at hand.

Try this: Build a culture in your classroom where the students feel comfortable calling on classmates. Rather than you always being the one to choose who will speak next, ask students to call on the fellow

student in the room with his hand up who has spoken the least during the conversation.

Pay careful attention to body language. Watch if one of your quieter students looks like he may have a point to bring up but feels shy raising his hand.

Let students know that their personal stories will be respected. Model the kind of behavior that you want them to have: "Sam, your story about the snake is fascinating. It shows me that you were really scared, and that you have worked to overcome your fear and learn more about this interesting creature." Acknowledge their feelings and look for positive opportunities to tie the comment into a shared moment of understanding for the class.

Whatever the age of your students, you are more likely to create a classroom that upholds values of respect and dignity if you lay out the ground rules for sharing information—from the very beginning of the year.

Turn students into self-teachers.

SEVENTEENTH CENTURY SCIENTIST and philosopher Galileo Galilei said, "You cannot teach a man anything, you can only help him find it within himself."

I've developed a system to help students become their own teachers. Here's how it works:

The students record their three best achievements on a particular assignment and the three things they most need to work on. When the next assignment rolls around, students take out their lists and write at the top of the new assignment which skills they plan to work on. I ask them to choose a very specific type of skill—an organizational principle, applying evidence, etc.

Even a second-grade student can take a moment after a math test to write down how well she thinks she has performed, and what she needs to work on the most next week.

The end result? Students are more focused and responsible for their own work. They're learning from their mistakes in a positive way. And I gain a starting point for what to look for on their next assignment.

Think of correcting assignments as feeding information to your students. When you give a student a fish, you feed her for a day; when you teach a student to fish, you feed her for a lifetime.

Invite in the administration.

FOR MOST OF us, it's nerve-racking to have an administrator observe you, even if you've been teaching for years.

After a few years of teaching, I still felt as nervous as ever. So I developed a new strategy—inviting my supervisor to watch me teach on *my* schedule. I chose lesson plans I was proud of, and then asked my supervisor to observe me teaching that class. I asked her to pay special attention to an area I knew needed improvement: how to include all students in group discussions. She accepted my invitation and when the day came for her observation, I felt more

An Invitation
to
My Class

comfortable because I was ready. After watching me teach the class, she offered some positive feedback as well as specific tips on handling discussions. I felt like I was part of a team with a coach there to guide me.

Evaluation can and should be a helpful process. View your administration as a resource to make you a better teacher.

Keep them on their toes.

IN TRADITIONAL AFRO-CARIBBEAN storytelling, the storyteller renews the audience's attention by periodically calling out "Crick!" and the audience responds with "Crack!" The shared interaction keeps the audience actively involved in the story.

How can this translate in your classroom?

It's going to depend a lot on your individual style. You can try startling them by suddenly altering your voice (this is where I'll stoop to anything, even singing). You can stop giving directions part way through a series of tasks and ask a random student to try to guess what comes next. You can try suddenly moving to a new place in the room without warning and then asking everybody else to move, too, for a new perspective. You can even ask students to stand up and do a jumping jack after they've heard one of their weekly vocabulary words used in the middle of class time. Each student will try her hardest not to be the last to jump out of her chair.

Physical and verbal interruptions in class might cause brief chaos, but they will help keep the students involved.

Crick! Crack!

Give rewards.

MY FIFTH-GRADE teacher, Mr. Anderson, understood bribery. In a good way! *If* we were good all week, and *if* we had done well enough on our Thursday math quiz, we would be allowed to play math bingo on Friday. Looking back, it was just another game like the ones we'd played for math practice all week. But the fact that this particular one was only given to us on Fridays raised its value inestimably in our eyes. Our teacher took away the "privilege" often enough to keep us on our toes and wanting more. It didn't hurt, either, that he threw in a special prize for the winner, which usually consisted of a good conduct star or a sticker and included the

much-sought-after Big Pumpkin Award on Halloween (a pumpkin so large that it had to be delivered to the winner's home by the teacher). Math suddenly became the most important topic at school; we couldn't get enough of it.

I've discovered that rewards large and small go a long ways towards building class morale and community—and yes, even high school students will compete enthusiastically for stickers! One firm tradition I keep in class is time for independent reading and teatime for half an hour on Fridays—*if* we've gotten the week's work done, and *if* they can prove to me that they're immersed in their books. It works! Even reluctant readers feel that they're gaining a special reward. I make a point of reading alongside them and chatting with them about their latest selections to emphasize that I think it's fun, too!

Visual-ize!

IN MY FIRST year of teaching, I often gave my students final reminders before the end of class. One ninth grader, Jesse, raised his hand. "I'd remember it better if you wrote it down," he said.

Such a simple idea. But I'd completely forgotten to do it.

There will be many kinds of learners in your classroom. Many, or even most, will learn well through visual examples. Make time to put critical examples on the board. Most students benefit from those visual cues that accompany oral instructions.

Design lesson plans where your students share the critical information on the board. Keep a record of written comments or ideas up front where they can see them. Even better, accompany the words with drawings. Let them work in small groups and then ask them to aid their peers by drawing simple cartoons illustrating a math point, such as how to add fractions. When it's review time, ask the students to think back to those visual representations. "Remember Ada's picture of the pineapple pizza?"

You'll be amazed how much more they remember next time around!

Ask for student input.

MANY SCHOOLS ASK students to fill out written evaluations at the end of the semester to give the teacher suggestions on how to tweak a class for next time. But what about right now? Doesn't today's class also deserve a teacher's best?

I remember one end-of-year evaluation from a student that suggested she would have performed better research if I had given several small assignments for practice finding sources at regular intervals. Great information—but it came too late for me to help that particular student. And she had not had the confidence to seek me out during the year.

But what if I had given her (and all my students) the opportunity to give me feedback earlier?

Don't be afraid to ask students of any age for feedback at regular intervals.

For younger students, ask them at the end of the unit to describe to you which activities helped them to learn the most. Give them a list of the activities you did to jog their memories. For older students, you might give them a short questionnaire on Fridays, asking which activities that week helped them learn best and what might help them to learn better. Let students know when you have found their comments particularly helpful.

It's one more way to gain students' trust and appreciation—and a way to improve your craft based on the feedback of those who spend the time with you.

Be a student.

MAKE TIME EVERY year to learn about new ideas that you care about, whether going to a conference about new ideas in technology, learning about ways to help solve a local crisis with the environment, studying a new language, or pursuing a side interest in art by taking a life-drawing class. If you don't have time for a course, try checking a few books out of the library on a favorite subject at the start of vacation. Go to a one-day seminar on Civil War history. Get your imagination going and your neurons firing.

As busy as you may be with planning and grading, not to mention with all of the necessities of an adult life, like childcare and paying bills, it's hard to make time to take classes on your own. You may have some external motivators encouraging you to do so: your school may encourage or require that you pursue professional development in education. But what about subjects outside of your discipline, personal passions that may be on the periphery of what is truly necessary to your job?

When you are alive to new ideas, you might gain some intriguing ways to create an interdisciplinary activity in your classroom. For example, instead of asking fourteen-year-old students to write a paper about the first act of *Romeo and Juliet*, I capitalize on my side interest in costume design by asking them to visually represent relationships between the characters through color and line. This is something I like to study in my spare time.

At the very least, your students will love hearing about your side interests and studies. They'll respect you for being a student, too, and you'll empathize with them more, making you a better teacher.

RULE
52

Keep it positive.

COMPARE THESE TWO experiences in music class. The first teacher stops the students frequently to tell them when they are out of tune, when they have held a note too long, when they have interrupted a phrase with a breath in the wrong place. The second teacher lets the students sing the piece through. She gives them praise for their focus and for the improvement of the quality of sound. Then she goes back and asks students to work on phrasing throughout the piece.

Which class would you rather be in? And which class do you think would sound better at the end of the period?

You got it—the class with the enthusiastic, positive teacher.

Even if your students have sixteen things wrong with the product they're trying to accomplish, don't forget to start with praise. What did they do that worked well? Start there, and then pick one or two things to concentrate on. If the students are overwhelmed, or if they begin to feel that their efforts don't matter in the big picture, they'll feel discouraged and lose interest.

And if you stay focused on the positives, you'll enjoy the class more, too!

YOU GOTTA KNOW THE
Rules!

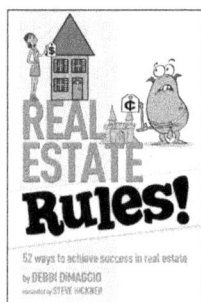

www.ingramcontent.com/pod-product-compliance
Lightning Source LLC
Chambersburg PA
CBHW052125090426

42741CB00009B/1959